MW01170404

European History for Kids

Vol. 2

A Captivating Guide to the History of Europe
from the Age of Enlightenment through the
Industrial Revolution to the 21st Century

Table of Contents

INTRODUCTION

In this book, you will explore the important historical events that took place from the end of the 18th century right through to today. In a relatively short amount of time, Europe has undergone many significant changes, including two world wars, numerous revolutions, and more. You will be amazed at the resilience and bravery of the European people.

Fun Fact: Europe is the second-smallest continent. It is made up of 44 different countries and is home to nearly 750 million people.

History will come alive in this book with fun facts, activities, and images. We've also included helpful pronunciation tips for those tricky new words!

If you haven't read Volume 1 of our European History for Kids yet, be sure to check it out to discover what Europe was like from prehistoric times to the 17th century.

Chapter 1: The Age of Enlightenment

The Age of Enlightenment was a philosophical movement that spread throughout Europe and the rest of the world during the 18th century. The main concept of the movement was the idea that people should think for themselves using logic and reasoning.

Fun Fact: The Enlightenment is also referred to as the Age of Reason.

The people of the Enlightenment did not like the power that the monarchy and church had over the people. They felt that all people were equal. If everyone was educated the same, then society would be fairer. They were also firm believers in using science and reason to find answers instead of relying on just religion. They wanted freedom of religion so people could decide for themselves what they believed in.

Because the philosophers during the Age of Enlightenment objected to the total control that the kings and the Roman Catholic Church had over society, the monarchy and the church were worried. They banned many Enlightenment books and even arrested some philosophers. Despite their efforts, many people began thinking they should change the government and overthrow the kings and queens. They wanted to give the power back to the people.

There were many important figures in the movement. *John Locke* was an Englishman who is known as the father of *empiricism (uhm-pi-ruh-si-zm)*. This theory states that all knowledge comes from experience. He is also nicknamed the Father of *Liberalism (li-buh-ruh-li-zm)*. Liberalism is a political idea that promotes individual rights, civil liberties, free enterprise, and democracy.

A drawing of John Locke.
https://commons.wikimedia.org/w/index.php?curid=64390

The Enlightenment was especially important in France. Many French philosophers shaped the French Revolution. One philosopher was called *Voltaire*. He believed in *Deism (day-is-uhm)*. Deism is known as the "religion of nature." *Deists* believed that God exists but that he is only revealed to us through nature and reason, not through books and prophets. They rejected the idea of miracles and visions. Instead, they believed in what could be observed. Voltaire argued with the church and the French monarchy. He was eventually arrested and exiled from France.

Another important philosopher of the time was *Immanuel Kant*. He was perhaps the most influential person in the German Enlightenment. He is most famously known for his *Kantian ethics*. This was a set of strict moral principles that he believed should apply to all people. One of his beliefs was that you should always tell the truth, even if you could hurt someone's feelings or risk someone's life.

Fun Fact: Kant's last words before he died were "es ist gut," which means "it is good."

A drawing of Immanuel Kant.
https://commons.wikimedia.org/w/index.php?curid=89082292

The Enlightenment sparked many big changes throughout Europe, including the French Revolution. The concept eventually fizzled out in favor of new ideas, such as *Romanticism*. Romanticism appealed more to the common less-educated people. It favored art, music, and literature instead of science and technology.

Chapter 1 Challenge Activity

Can you fill in the blanks?

The Age of _____ was a philosophical movement that believed in rational thinking using logic and reasoning. The movement did not like the fact that the monarchy and the _____ had total control over the people. They thought people should be treated _____ . They believed in science, reason, and religious freedom.

John Locke was the father of empiricism, the idea that all knowledge comes from _____ . He is also known as the Father of _____ .

Another concept of this time was Deism, which is also called the religion of _____ .

Immanuel Kant came up with the _____ ethics, a strict set of moral principles. One of the principles was the idea that you should always _____ , even if it hurts someone.

The Age of Enlightenment was a philosophical movement that believed in rational thinking using logic and reasoning. The movement did not like the fact that the monarchy and the Catholic Church had total control over the people. They thought people should be treated equally. They believed in science, reason, and religious freedom.

John Locke was the father of empiricism, the idea that all knowledge comes from experience. He is also known as the Father of Liberalism.

Another concept of this time was Deism, which is also called the religion of nature.

Immanuel Kant came up with the Kantian Ethics, a strict set of moral principles. One of the principles was the idea that you should always tell the truth, even if it hurts someone.

Chapter 2: The Industrial Revolution

During the late 18th century, Great Britain underwent *the Industrial Revolution*. During the Industrial Revolution, the manufacturing of products began to happen on a larger scale in factories. The revolution then spread farther into Europe and the United States. The Industrial Revolution led to new technologies and a huge cultural shift. Many people flocked to the cities for work. Before this, people had mostly lived and worked in the countryside on farms. Because of the large factories and vast numbers of people arriving, the cities became overcrowded, polluted, and dirty.

The first industry that was revolutionized was the cloth industry. Previously, wool had to be gathered, spun into yarn, and woven by hand to make fabric. In 1733, the *flying shuttle* was invented, which made weaving much easier. In 1770, the *spinning jenny* was invented to easily spin yarn. In 1793, the *cotton gin* was invented by *Eli Whitney* to clean freshly picked cotton. Whitney went on to discover that machines could create many parts of a product at once. These parts could then easily be assembled by workers, allowing goods to be created far more quickly.

Factories produced a number of different goods. The Industrial Revolution saw an increase in coal mines, steel mills, cotton mills, and more.

Another important invention that impacted factories was the invention of the steam engine, which powered machines. The Industrial Revolution also led to the invention of new machines to help with agriculture and farming. Because of the new demand for large-scale production, improvements to transportation were made. Before, people traveled by foot or on horseback. The people wanted a quicker and easier way to transport raw materials and finished products. The steamboat was perfected in 1807 by *Robert Fulton*. The steam *locomotive* engine for railroads was invented by *George Stephenson* in 1825.

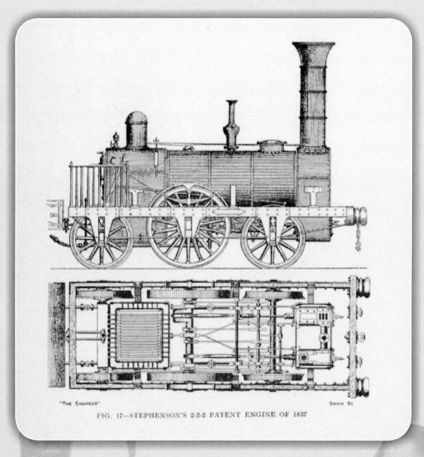

FIG. 17—STEPHENSON'S 2-2-2 PATENT ENGINE OF 1837

A patent for a locomotive engine by Stephenson in 1837.

The working conditions during the Industrial Revolution were poor. People had to work very long hours. They could be fired if they were sick or injured and unable to work. There were no laws in place to protect workers. Unlike today, a six-day workweek and twelve--hour days were normal. The jobs were often dangerous. Many of the machines had no safety features, so it was not unusual for people to lose a finger or limb at work.

It was no better in the mines either. The tunnels could collapse, and the conditions were very hot, uncomfortable, and dark. The air in the factories and mines was very poor, making it difficult to breathe. It even caused diseases like cancer. Many factories required workers to handle flammable chemicals that could cause fires or explosions. Girls would work in match factories. The chemical they used, *phosphorous (fo-sfuh-ruhs)*, would cause their teeth to fall out.

Children were expected to work in the same conditions as adults. Children as young as four years old would work full-time to help provide for their families. Many businesses preferred to hire children since they were cheaper and could fit into the tight spaces between machines.

Fun Fact: On average, children were paid 10 to 20 percent of what adults earned.

Children commonly worked in the mines or as chimney sweeps. They also sold newspapers. Some children weren't even paid for working. Instead, they were given food and board. Because they spent so much time working, many children were unable to go to school. Because of the increase in demand for child labor, women were expected to have lots of children. It was not uncommon for families to have as many as ten children!

Pregnant women still had to work. Women would immediately return to work after giving birth, leaving their newborns with older family members.

A group of children working in a textile mill.
https://commons.wikimedia.org/w/index.php?curid=102595084

Because of the horrible working conditions, the workers eventually started to rebel. They joined together and formed unions. Unions fought for shorter hours, better working conditions, and higher wages. The unions would organize *strikes* (protests where people would stop working) to try to get the factory owners to give in to their demands.

One of the first labor laws to be passed was in Britain in 1819. The law said that it was illegal to hire children who were younger than nine years old. However, this was often ignored. There were even some early laws that made it illegal for workers to form unions (*unionize*).

Eventually, the unions became powerful. Working conditions improved, and more workers' laws and rights were granted.

Fun Fact: In 1888, thousands of matchgirls went on strike in London.

A drawing of women working in a match factory in London in 1871.
https://commons.wikimedia.org/w/index.php?curid=12538184

Chapter 2 Challenge Activity

1. Where did the Industrial Revolution start?

2. What three inventions revolutionized the cloth industry?

3. Which two inventions revolutionized transport?

4. At what age would some children start working?

5. Who organized work strikes?

Chapter 2 Answer

1. Where did the Industrial Revolution start? In Great Britain.

2. What three inventions revolutionized the cloth industry? The flying shuttle, spinning jenny, and cotton gin.

3. Which two inventions revolutionized transport? The steamboat and steam locomotive engine.

4. At what age would some children start working? Children as young as four would work full-time.

5. Who organized work strikes? Unions.

Chapter 3: The French Revolution

After the Age of Enlightenment, France underwent a revolution. The people of France overthrew the monarchy and government. The *French Revolution* lasted for ten years, from 1789 to 1799.

Before the French Revolution, France was ruled by a king. He had total control over the government and the people. France operated under a *hierarchical (hai-uh-raa-kuh-kl)* society. People were separated into different social classes, known as *estates*. At the very top was the monarchy. Then, there was the *First Estate*, which was made up of people from the church. The *Second Estate* was made up of noblemen, and the *Third Estate* was the common folk. The majority of people who lived in France were part of the Third Estate.

During the French Revolution, the Third Estate rose up against the ruling estates. This happened because of several different reasons. Firstly, the French government was in debt. This was partly due to the lavish lifestyle the king enjoyed. France had also borrowed money to fight the British in the Seven Years' War and to aid the Americans in their revolution. To solve their debt problem, the government heavily taxed the poor Third Estate but not the wealthier people of the First and Second Estates. The common people were angry that they were paying more than their fair share.

Secondly, France experienced a famine in 1789. Many commoners could barely afford to eat. They would eat bread to survive. However, the cost of bread greatly increased. The people began to starve.

A portrait of King Louis XVI.

Finally, the Age of Enlightenment meant that people's attitudes toward the church and monarchy had shifted. People realized there was an alternative to a monarchy. The Americans had shown that was possible with their revolution. The king of France, *King Louis XVI,* was also weakening in power. He did not realize how bad things were for the Third Estate, and he disagreed with the government over new reforms.

The Third Estate formed the *National Assembly* and asked King Louis to make changes. They demanded that the Third Estate should have more say in government. However, the Third Estate was concerned that the king was preparing his army instead of giving in to their demands.

The French Revolution started with the *Storming of the Bastille*. The Bastille was originally built as a fortress during the Hundred Years' War. By the 18th century, it had become a prison.

Fun Fact: July 14th (the day the Bastille was stormed) is celebrated as a national holiday in France. It is called Bastille Day.

A painting of the Storming of the Bastille.
https://commons.wikimedia.org/w/index.php?curid=106405

Around one thousand men from the Third Estate stormed the Bastille. They were tradesmen and store owners with little to no military experience. They decided to attack the Bastille because it was home to political prisoners. The Bastille had also become symbolic of the king's oppression of the people.

Before storming the Bastille, they knew they would need weapons. They first took over the *Hotel des Invalides (an·vuh·leed)*, where they found guns. Once the fighting broke out, the Bastille's leader, *Governor de Launey (law-neeh)*, realized they would not win and surrendered. Although he and his men surrendered, Governor de Launey was beheaded. His head was carried through the celebrating streets of Paris on a spike. This success triggered many more uprisings in France.

Fun Fact: **There were only seven prisoners in the Bastille when it was stormed. All of them were freed by the revolutionaries.**

Another important event during the French Revolution is known as the *Women's March on Versailles*. This occurred on October 5th, 1789. A group of women went to the market to buy bread to feed their starving families. They soon found there was very little bread available. The bread being sold was too expensive. The women began to march, demanding fairer prices so they could feed their families. As they marched, more women joined the protest. Soon, there were thousands of people.

The crowd marched to *Hotel de Ville (vil)*, where they found some bread and weapons. Then, they decided to march on the palace in Versailles, where the king and his wife, Queen *Marie Antoinette (an-twuh-net)*, were. The angry crowd marched for six hours in the pouring rain to reach the palace.

When they arrived, the king agreed to meet with a few of the women and promised them some food from his own stores. However, not all of the revolutionaries were happy with this and continued to protest. Eventually, the crowd broke into the palace and killed some guards before order was restored by the leader of the National Guard, *Marquis de Lafayette (maa-kwuhs du lah-fi-et)*.

The crowd demanded Marie Antoinette come out to speak with them. Many people disliked her for her lavish spending. It is likely that the crowd intended to kill her. She knew this, so when she came out, she brought her children with her. The crowd realized this was a ploy and demanded the children be sent back inside. Luckily for Marie Antoinette, Marquis de Lafayette calmed the situation by kneeling at her feet and kissing her hand. Afterward, the king and queen traveled back to Paris as prisoners with the crowd, which had grown from seven thousand people to sixty thousand!

A painting of Marie Antoinette.

Two years after the king and queen were captured, they attempted to flee France in what is known as the *Flight to Varennes*. However, they were found and returned to Paris, where they were later executed. King Louis was executed first in January 1793. Marie Antoinette was executed later that year. She was one of the first casualties of the *Reign of Terror*.

The Reign of Terror saw radicals led by *Maximilien Robespierre (row-buhz-peeuh)* take control of the government. Robespierre was a member of a group called the *Jacobins* who believed the revolution should be protected at all costs. On September 5th, 1793, Robespierre declared that terror would be "the order of the day." Anyone suspected of not being loyal to the revolution would be arrested and executed by *guillotine (gi-luh-teen)*. A guillotine was a type of machine with a heavy blade at the top. The person would put their head into it, and the blade would be dropped, beheading them.

People were very scared. They had to be careful about what they said since being accused often led to death. Revolutionaries would often accuse someone they didn't like or wanted out of the way. On July 27th, 1794, Robespierre was overthrown. The Reign of Terror had ended, and Robespierre was executed the next day.

Soldiers in the French Revolution.
https://commons.wikimedia.org/w/index.php?curid=5277417

Toward the end of the French Revolution, the government of France, the *Directory*, began to weaken. This led to a new government known as the *Consulate*. The Consulate was led by a Jacobian military leader named *Napoleon Bonaparte (nuh-pow-lee-uhn bow-nuh-paat)*. He would go on to become the dictator of France. (A dictator is a ruler who has total power and often gains it by using force.) He introduced many reforms, including the *Napoleonic Code*. The Napoleonic Code said that people in government could not be appointed because of their birth or religion. Instead, they had to be qualified for the position.

Under Napoleon's rule, France extended its territories. At its peak, the First French Empire took up much of Europe, from Spain to the Russian border. However, Napoleon's army was unsuccessful in their attempt to conquer Britain in the *Battle of Trafalgar*. Napoleon also made a fateful mistake when he tried to invade Russia. Many of his soldiers starved to death or from the cold weather on the journey to and from Russia. They found the city of Moscow abandoned when they arrived. Having lost most of his men on the doomed trip to Russia, Napoleon was weak. He was attacked by the rest of Europe. He was eventually defeated in the *Battle of Waterloo* on June 18th, 1815, and forced into exile.

BONAPARTE.

A drawing of Napoleon Bonaparte.

Fun Fact: Napoleon is famously known for being short. However, he was five foot six inches, which was an average height at the time. The idea of him being short is so ingrained in our culture that people often refer to someone as having a "Napoleon complex" if they are overcompensating (an overaction to being less superior than others) for being short.

Fun Fact: France wasn't the only European country to undergo a revolution during this time. The Serbian Revolution took place in Serbia between 1804 to 1835 against the Ottoman Empire. The Greek Revolution began in 1821 when the people of Greece fought for their independence from the Ottoman Empire.

Chapter 3 Challenge Activity

1. What event is considered to be the start of the French Revolution?
   a. The Storming of the Bastille
   b. The Women's March on Versailles
   c. The Reign of Terror

2. Who was rumored to have said "let them eat cake" when asked what the poor should do without bread?
   a. Louis XVI
   b. Napoleon Bonaparte
   c. Marie Antoinette

3. What was the common method of execution during the Reign of Terror?
   a. Hanging
   b. Guillotine
   c. Electric chair

4. What were the common people of France known as during this time?
   a. The First Estate
   b. The Second Estate
   c. The Third Estate

5. Who became the first emperor of France after the end of the French Revolution?
   a. Napoleon Bonaparte
   b. Maximilien Robespierre
   c. Marquis de Lafayette

1. What event is considered to be the start of the French Revolution?

   a. The Storming of the Bastille

2. Who was rumored to have said "let them eat cake" when asked what the poor should do without bread?

   c. Marie Antoinette

3. What was the common method of execution during the Reign of Terror?

   b. Guillotine

4. What were the common people of France known as during this time?

   c. The Third Estate

5. Who became the first emperor of France after the end of the French Revolution?

   a. Napoleon Bonaparte

Chapter 4: World War I

In this chapter, we will discuss a sad period in European history. The First World War took place between 1914 and 1918. World War I is also referred to as WWI, the Great War, and the war to end all wars.

Fun Fact: WWI was fought on two fronts. The Western Front was along the coast of Belgium to Switzerland. The Eastern Front was in Eastern Europe and spread from the Baltic Sea to the Black Sea.

The First World War is known as a world war because many countries fought in it. The two sides were known as the *Central Powers* and the *Allied Powers*. The Central Powers were Germany, the Ottoman Empire, Bulgaria, and Austria-Hungary (also known as the *Austro-Hungarian Empire*). The Allied Powers (the Allies) were the UK, Russia, and France. In 1917, the US also joined the Allied Powers.

Before the war, many powerful countries in Europe were making alliances and trying to gain power. In 1882, Germany, Italy, and Austria-Hungary formed the *Triple Alliance*. They agreed to fight for each other if France attacked one of them. However, Italy went against the alliance. It made a secret alliance with France against Germany. France also made an agreement with Russia in 1892 and Britain in 1904. Finally, in 1907, France, Russia, and Britain formed a three-way alliance called the *Triple Entente (on-tont)*. Germany felt very threatened by the Triple Entente.

A map of military alliances in 1914.

(By historicair (French original) Fluteflute & User:Bibi Saint-Pol (English translation), CC BY-SA 2.5 <https://creativecommons.org/licenses/by-sa/2.5>, via Wikimedia Commons, https://commons.wikimedia.org/w/index.php?curid=5702671)

These alliances caused a lot of competition between countries. In addition, countries like France and Britain had established large *imperial (im-peeuh-ree-uhl)* empires. Germany and Russia wanted empires of their own. All of this distrust and jealousy meant that Europe was primed for war. It wouldn't take much to spark it.

As with many wars, there are a lot of complicated reasons behind why World War I took place. However, one event triggered the start of the Great War: the assassination of *Archduke Franz Ferdinand.* Ferdinand was the heir to the Austro-Hungarian throne. On June 28th, 1914, he was assassinated in *Sarajevo (sa-ruh-yay-vow),* Bosnia. At the time, Bosnia was part of Austria-Hungary. Many Bosnians wanted independence. A group of Bosnian radicals plotted Ferdinand's assassination. With help from the *Black Hand*, a secret military group from Serbia, the group known as the *Young Bosnians* were able to successfully assassinate Franz Ferdinand.

Fun Fact: The Young Bosnians made two attempts to assassinate Ferdinand that day. The first attempt was by a man named Nedeljko Cabrinovic (ne-del-ko kah-brin-oh-vik). He threw a bomb at Ferdinand's car, but it bounced off it. The second attempt was by Gavrilo Princip (guh-vri-low prin-sip), who shot both Ferdinand and his wife.

While it is still widely debated whether the Serbian government had any involvement in the assassination, Austria-Hungary believed they did. It declared war on Serbia. Russia was allied with Serbia and began to gather its troops to help them. Germany declared war on Russia to help its ally Austria-Hungary. France then got involved and

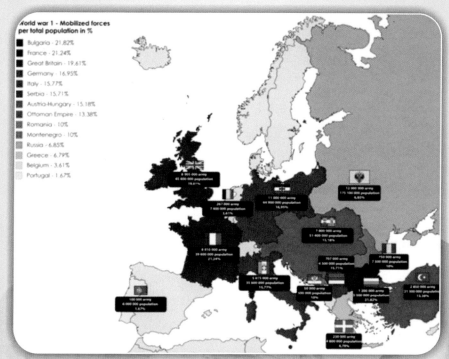

A map of the percentage of mobilized forces per total population in WWI.

declared war on Germany. Germany invaded Belgium to advance on France, which led Britain to declare war on Germany. All these declarations of war happened within just a few days of each other. On July 28th, 1914, World War I officially began.

Fun Fact: Almost eight million men from Austria-Hungary fought in WWI. Ninety percent of these soldiers were either wounded or killed.

The majority of the fighting was done in trenches. This kind of fighting is known as *trench warfare*. Trenches are long and narrow. They are dug deep into the ground and run for many miles. Trenches made it incredibly difficult for either side to gain ground. Neither side was able to advance for the majority of the war.

Fun Fact: The ground between the trenches was 150 to 750 feet apart. It was nicknamed "no man's land." It was often boobytrapped with landmines and barbed wire.

Conditions in the trenches were not pleasant. They were infested with rats, frogs, and lice. The lice caused the soldiers to get *trench fever*. The rats ate a lot of their food and even the poor soldiers if they could! The trenches could flood. The mud would clog their weapons, making it hard to move around in battle. The soldiers could never get dry, which caused them to get *trench foot*. They had to amputate their toes or feet if their trench foot was severe. If they didn't lose their toes to trench foot, they risked losing them to frostbite when it was cold.

The soldiers dug the trenches in three different ways. *Entrenching* was where they dug straight into the ground. *Sapping* was where they extended a trench from within. *Tunneling* was where they would build a tunnel and then remove the roof. Tunneling was the safest but hardest method. The next safest was sapping, but it was slow. The quickest but most dangerous method was entrenching. This method left the soldiers open to enemy fire.

The average soldier in the trenches would have a hand grenade, a rifle, and a *bayonet*–a type of knife that could attach to the end of a rifle to be used as a spear in close combat.

Fun Fact: Dogs were a fast and reliable way to carry messages within the trenches.

A photo of some soldiers in the trenches.
https://commons.wikimedia.org/w/index.php?curid=486069

Lots of different battles were fought throughout World War I. One of the first was the *Battle of Tannenberg (ta-nuhn-buhg)*. This battle was fought between the German and Russian armies on German soil. The Germans emerged victorious from the battle. They almost completely decimated (wiped out) the Russian Second Army. Of over 200,000 Russian soldiers, 50,000 were killed. One hundred thousand were captured.

Over in France, two battles were fought: the *First Battle of the Marne (mar-nee)* in 1914 and the *Second Battle of the Marne* in 1918. The French and the British successfully held off the Central Powers during the first battle, although they suffered heavy losses.

Fun Fact: The First Battle of the Marne was the first time reconnaissance planes were used to discover an enemy's position.

Another important battle during WWI was the *Battle of the Somme (som)*. It took place between the Allied Powers and the German Empire in 1916. Both sides engaged in trench warfare for two years after the First Battle of the Marne. Neither side had gained much ground. The British and French armies decided to attack near the Somme to push the Germans out of France. However, their plan did not work out as expected. The Germans launched the *Battle of Verdun (vur-dun)*. The Allies began their plan, hoping that it would divert the Germans away from Verdun.

At the Somme, the Allies bombarded the Germans for eight days, firing millions of rounds of ammunition. However, the Germans had been warned of the attack and took shelter. The Allies did not inflict much damage. The Allied commanders did not listen when they were told their bombardment was unsuccessful. On July 1st, they ordered their men to advance. Their soldiers were easily shot down by the unharmed enemy forces. The Allies suffered over twenty thousand casualties. Sixty thousand men were injured on the first day of the Battle of the Somme, making it the worst day in the history of British warfare. But that didn't stop the Allies. They continued to advance until November 18th. They had suffered 600,000 casualties and only gained 7 miles of territory. This means the Allied Powers lost approximately eighty-nine thousand men for every mile they gained.

Fun Fact: With over one million casualties between both sides, the Battle of the Somme is one of the most catastrophic battles in history.

On April 6th, 1917, the United States declared war on Germany and became a part of the Allied Powers. This was largely because Germany had tried to convince Mexico to become its ally and join the war. Shortly after this, in November, the Russian Revolution began. The Russian army agreed to peace with the Central Powers and withdrew from the war a month later.

In January 1918, US President *Woodrow Wilson* came up with his *Fourteen Points* statement. He wanted to achieve peace and end the war. The German Army launched a last-ditch attack on the Allies before the US troops could arrive. However, the US forces had arrived by the Second Battle of the Marne. The Allied Powers defeated the Central Powers. Four months later, on November 11th, 1918, the exhausted Germans admitted defeat and agreed to an *armistice (aa-muh-stuhs)*. An armistice is where both sides agree to a *ceasefire (sees-fai-uh)*, a temporary pause in the fighting. With the agreement in place and a treaty ready to be signed, the Allies emerged as the winners of the First World War.

Fun Fact: Although the war is considered to have ended when the fighting stopped, it didn't officially end until June 28th, 1919, when the Treaty of Versailles was signed.

The signing of the Treaty of Versailles.
https://commons.wikimedia.org/w/index.php?curid=22842011)

Fun Fact: The soldiers who survived the war would suffer "shell shock," now known as PTSD. The horrors of war had a lasting effect on them. Men would suffer mental and physical issues, such as uncontrollable shaking, nightmares, exhaustion, and more.

Chapter 4 Challenge Activity

Can you spot which of the following sentences are true and which are false?

1. WWI started because Archduke Franz
   Ferdinand was assassinated.   TRUE/FALSE

2. Germany and the Central Powers won the war.   TRUE/FALSE

3. World War I is considered to have ended on November
   11th, 1918, when the fighting stopped.   TRUE/FALSE

4. The first day of the Battle of Tannenberg was the
   worst day in the history of British warfare.   TRUE/FALSE

5. A large portion of the fighting during WWI took
   place in the trenches and is known as trench warfare.   TRUE/FALSE

Chapter 4 Answer

Can you spot which of the below sentences are true or false?

1. WWI started because Archduke Franz Ferdinand was assassinated. TRUE

2. Germany and the Central Powers won the war. FALSE The Allies won the war.

3. World War I is considered to have ended on November 11th, 1918, when the fighting stopped. TRUE (Although it officially ended on June 28th, 1919, with the signing of the Treaty of Versailles.)

4. The first day of the Battle of Tannenberg was the worst day in the history of British warfare. FALSE (The first day of the Battle of the Somme was the worst day in the history of British warfare.)

5. A large portion of the fighting during WWI took place in the trenches and is known as trench warfare. TRUE

Chapter 5: Women's Suffrage

The *women's suffrage (suh-fruhj) movement* was a movement for women to be allowed the right to vote. This movement took place all over the world at different times since many countries did not allow women to vote. Throughout history, laws have been put in place preventing people from voting. For years, many thought that women did not deserve the right to vote.

Fun Fact: Queen Victoria of Britain was against women getting the vote, describing it as a "mad, wicked folly."

Europe is made up of many different countries. Each of them had its own rules. The first women in Europe to demand the right to vote were the women of France during the French Revolution. However, it wasn't until the end of the 19th century and into the 20th century that most of the movements really began to take off.

Fun Fact: Sweden was far ahead of its European neighbors. Laws existed that allowed women to vote back in the 1700s!

Perhaps the most famous women's suffrage movement in Europe was in Great Britain. In Britain, during the late 1800s and early 1900s, there were two main groups. There were the *National Union of Women's Suffrage Societies*, nicknamed the *Suffragists (suh-fruh-jists)*, and the *Women's Social and Political Union* or *Suffragettes*. The groups both wanted the same thing. They wanted women to be given the right to vote, but they used very different methods to achieve it.

During the height of the movement (1890-1919), *Millicent Garrett Fawcett* led the Suffragists. The Suffragists only wanted women who were middle class and owned property to get the right to vote. They used peaceful protests to try and achieve this. Their tactics made good progress. Some proposed bills for women's suffrage had gained some support by 1900.

However, one of the Suffragist members, *Emmeline Pankhurst*, was unhappy with their progress. She wanted a more radical approach. She formed her own society, the Suffragettes. The Suffragettes were more open to women. The Suffragettes did not include just the middle and upper classes. After 1905, the Suffragettes became increasingly violent. They would handcuff themselves to railings, go on hunger strikes, break windows, and even plant bombs. Because of

Photo of Emmeline Pankhurst being arrested outside Buckingham Palace while trying to present a petition to King George V in May 1914.
https://commons.wikimedia.org/w/index.php?curid=30905246

their extreme methods, Suffragettes would often be arrested. If they went on a hunger strike while in prison, they would be force-fed or even released until they began eating again. They would then be rearrested under *the Cat and Mouse Act.*

Fun Fact: The Suffragettes' motto was "Deeds not words."

The police were rather harsh toward the Suffragettes. The Suffragettes began to gain support, especially after one of their members tragically died after being trampled by the king's racehorse. Emily Wilding Davison stepped out in front of the horse during a race at Epsom in protest and was trampled.

Then, WWI broke out. Women were significantly impacted. The leaders of the Suffragettes and Suffragists stopped campaigning and encouraged women to focus on the war effort. Before the war, people saw a woman's place in the home. During the war, the majority of young men were off fighting. The women had to work.

Women were provided with more independence, which helped push reforms through Parliament. In 1918, the British government passed a bill that allowed some women to vote. Women who were over thirty years old and owned property or were married to someone who did could vote. Over eight million women in the UK could finally vote!

Fun Fact: It took another ten years for all women in Britain to be granted the same voting rights as men.

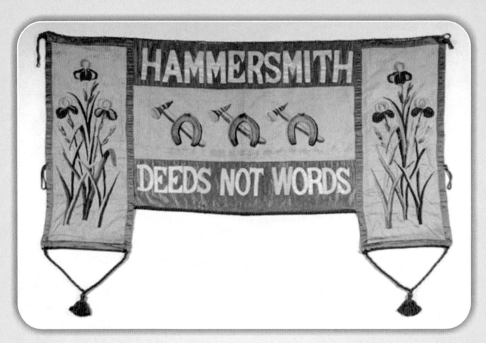

Suffragettes' banner.

Chapter 5 Challenge Activity

Can you match these facts with the correct political party nickname?

Suffragettes	Suffragists

Used violent protests, including hunger strikes and planting bombs

Women's Social and Political Union

National Union of Women's Suffrage Societies

Led by Emmeline Pankhurst

Believed in peaceful protest

Had the motto "Deeds not words"

Led by Millicent Garrett Fawcett

Only wanted the vote for certain women

Suffragettes	Suffragists
Women's Social and Political Union	National Union of Women's Suffrage Societies
Used violent protests, including hunger strikes and planting bombs	Believed in peaceful protest
Had the motto "Deeds not words"	Only wanted the vote for certain women
Led by Emmeline Pankhurst	Led by Millicent Garrett Fawcett

Chapter 6: The Great Depression

If you've heard the word depression before, chances are you think of someone who is very sad. However, there is another meaning for the word. Depression also refers to a long and particularly bad economic *recession* (where the economy suffers a big decline).

The Great Depression began in 1929 and ended in 1939. It was the longest and worst depression ever experienced in the industrialized Western world. It started in the United States, where there was a huge crash in the stock market. Although it may have started in the US, the Great Depression was felt by almost every country in the world.

Fun Fact: The Wall Street stock market crash on October 29th, 1929, is known as Black Tuesday. Many people lost their entire life savings and became unemployed or even homeless. This crash set off a chain of events that led to a ten-year economic recession throughout the world.

A crowd gathered outside of the New York Stock Exchange on Black Tuesday.

When the Great Depression started, Europe was still recovering from the First World War. Europe had suffered huge losses. The countries had lost many people. They also had to rebuild due to the damage caused to factories, homes, and transport systems. By the middle of the 1920s, many European countries had finally rebuilt much of what had been lost. The population was also on the rise.

However, the European economy did not bounce back so quickly. While the Europeans were at war, countries like Japan and the US had grown richer and taken over many trade opportunities. The US workers were producing more goods more quickly thanks to new technology. European businesses struggled to regain a foothold in these markets after the war.

It wasn't just manufacturing that the US market had a monopoly (exclusive control) over. It was also able to provide superior *produce* (food grown at farms) at lower prices. This hit the eastern European countries especially hard. Agriculture made up 70 percent of their income. The peace treaties following the war also made it very difficult for the Central Powers to bounce back. They were forbidden from working together and had to pay *reparations* (compensation the defeated side paid for war damages) to the European Allies.

When the Great Depression hit America, it also affected Europe. The American loans that had bolstered Europe's economy were no longer available.

Fun Fact: In 1931, the US invested nothing in Europe.

The countries that struggled the most during the Great Depression were Germany, Austria, and Poland. Their industrial output dropped 40 percent, and one in five people were unemployed. European trade was hugely impacted. Many banks were on the brink of collapse.

The economic uncertainty led to political unrest. More extreme political parties began to win votes when governments failed to resolve the economic crisis. Relationships between various European countries also worsened. Everyone began to "take care of their own" and protect their own best interests. Countries like Italy and Germany saw these new *nationalist* ideals as a way to expand their empires. They applied the ideals to politics and economics.

Fun Fact: A nationalist often supports their own nation's interests by excluding or harming other nations' interests. They also believe their nation should self-govern (rule itself) without outside interference.

Benito Mussolini (mu-suh-lee-nee) of the *National Fascist Party* in Italy and *Adolf Hitler* of the *Nazi Party* in Germany started to expand their territories into eastern Europe, the Mediterranean, and Africa. The previously strong European countries of Britain and France felt weak. They struggled to cooperate and the US due to competition over resources. This undoubtedly contributed to the political climate that led Europe into the *Second World War*.

A photo of Mussolini and Hitler in 1940.
https://commons.wikimedia.org/w/index.php?curid=41283482

Chapter 6 Challenge Activity

1. When did the Great Depression take place?

2. Where did the Great Depression start?

3. Which European countries struggled the most?

4. Which nationalist leaders tried to expand their empires during this time?

Chapter 6 Answer

1. When did the Great Depression take place? Between 1929 and 1939

2. Where did the Great Depression start? In the United States of America

3. Which European countries struggled the most? Germany, Austria, and Poland

4. Which nationalist leaders tried to expand their empires during this time? Benito Mussolini and Adolf Hitler

Chapter 7: World War II

Twenty years after the end of the "war to end all wars," Europe took part in the Second World War. Like in WWI, the Allied Powers (the UK, France, the Soviet Union, and the US) would again be fighting Germany. However, this time Germany had new allies: Japan and Italy. They were known as the *Axis Powers*. Most of the world would become involved in the war in some way.

Fun Fact: WWII is the deadliest war in recorded history. Over seventy million people lost their lives during it.

A map of military alliances during WWII.

Men had no choice but to go to war during the world wars. Countries like the UK and the US *conscripted* (drafted) all healthy men of a certain age to fight. Men who refused to go to war would face imprisonment and were socially shunned.

Although women were not forced to fight, they were still very important for the war effort. Many worked as nurses or in non-combat areas of the army. The *Women's Army Corps*, or *WAC*, would help with communications and fixing vehicles. Women also flew planes under the *Women's Air Force Service Pilots* or *WASPs*. Most importantly, women went to work and kept factories running. Factories provided essential weapons, ammunition, and supplies for the war.

Women assembling armor-piercing shells in a factory during WWII.
https://commons.wikimedia.org/w/index.php?curid=530386

WWII Technology

The main weapons used during the Second World War were tanks, machine guns, warplanes, aircraft carrier ships that allowed planes to take off from anywhere, and different types of bombs. Most significantly, the atomic (or nuclear) bomb was invented.

Both sides created secret codes to keep their communications secret from the enemy. Mathematician Alan Turing cracked the German *Enigma code*. This gave the Allies a massive advantage since they could find out Germany's plans.

Fun Fact: All modern computers are based on Alan Turing's universal Turing machine's mathematical model.

Why WWII Started

As mentioned in our previous chapter, Hitler became the head of the Nazi Party and the *Führer (fure-er)* (leader) of Germany. Germany was known as the *Third Reich (rike)* at this time.

Fun Fact: Because the word Führer is typically associated with Hitler, German leaders are no longer called it.

Germany had been hit hard by the First World War and the Great Depression. The Germans were desperate for things to improve. Hitler did not like the restrictions placed upon Germany in the Treaty of Versailles. So, he allied with Benito Mussolini and began expanding Germany's empire. Because the Allies did not want another war, they tried using a method known as *appeasement*. They wanted to keep the peace by giving in to Hitler's demands through negotiations.

Germany and Italy used fascism (fa-shuh-zm) to rule. Fascist governments were led by dictators who violently suppressed anyone who opposed them. They had complete control and promoted nationalism and racism.

The appeasement approach meant Hitler and Mussolini could take over their neighbors. This encouraged Hitler to keep gaining more land until he took it too far and invaded Poland. Two days later, on September 3rd, 1939, Britain and France declared war on Germany.

Significant Moments of WWII

At the beginning of WWII, the Soviet Union was allied with Germany. Then, in 1940, Germany invaded several more European countries. In 1941, it invaded parts of the Soviet Union. By invading their territory, Germany lost the support of the Soviet Union. The Soviet Union aligned with the Allies instead. However, the Allies also lost an ally when Germany invaded France in 1940. The French surrendered to German *occupation* (when a military force occupies a country).

Initially, the United States tried to stay out of the war. But, on December 7th, 1941, the Japanese bombed *Pearl Harbor* in Hawaii. The US finally joined the fighting. They became integral in helping the Allies win.

By 1941, the Germans occupied and controlled most of Europe. However, they were perhaps too ambitious. They found themselves fighting on three fronts. The three fronts were the Eastern Front (Russia), the Mediterranean and African Front, and the Western Front (France and Britain).

In 1940, Germany tried to overtake Great Britain during what is known as the *Battle of Britain*. However, the British Royal Air Force proved to be too great an opponent. Germany could not invade

Britain, despite an extensive year-long bombing campaign on London known as *the Blitz*.

During the Blitz, the British government decided to evacuate children to the countryside, where it was safer. Thousands of *evacuees* were sent away from their parents to live with relatives or even complete strangers. Only mothers of children under five years old could go with their children. Approximately 3.5 million children were evacuated.

Fun Fact: Blackouts were introduced during the Blitz. Streetlights were switched off, and people had to cover their windows and drive without headlights so enemy bombers couldn't see them.

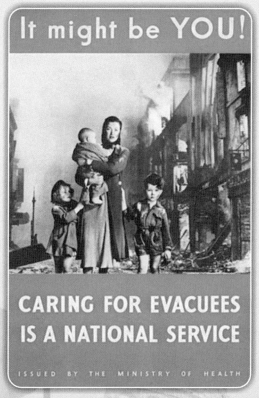

A poster encouraging people to take in evacuees during the Blitz.

https://commons.wikimedia.org/w/index.php?curid=30837035

In 1942 and 1943, the Allies went on the offensive. This means they were attacking instead of defending. The British bombed Germany. The Allies took control of North Africa, which allowed them to attack and defeat southern Italy. The Russians beat the German Army on the Eastern Front, causing them to retreat.

On June 6th, 1944, an event known as *D-Day* took place. The Allied Forces sent over 150,000 soldiers to the beaches of Normandy, France. The Allies successfully forced the Germans out of France. D-Day was a pivotal moment in the war.

Fun Fact: D-Day is also known as the Invasion of Normandy.

A photo of soldiers landing on Normandy Beach during D-Day.
https://commons.wikimedia.org/w/index.php?curid=43274

In retaliation for D-Day, the Germans launched what is known as the *Battle of the Bulge* in Belgium. The majority of the troops during this battle were from the US Army. The weather was very cold and snowy, and the US Army was caught off-guard by the unexpected attack. Even though the American troops were outnumbered, they successfully held off the Germans until reinforcements arrived. Together, they defeated the Germans.

Fun Fact: The Battle of the Bulge is considered one of the greatest battles ever fought by US soldiers.

Hitler realized the war was over. Instead of facing punishment for his crimes, he committed suicide on April 30th, 1945. On May 7th, 1945, Germany surrendered. The fighting in Europe was finally over. Massive celebrations were held throughout Allied Europe the next day.

Fun Fact: May 8th is known as V-E Day or Victory Day in Europe.

Although both Italy and Germany had surrendered, the Japanese continued to fight. America dropped two atomic bombs on the Japanese cities of Hiroshima and Nagasaki. Japan finally surrendered on September 2nd, 1945.

Winston Churchill

In 1940, Britain elected a new prime minister, *Winston Churchill*. Unlike his predecessor, Churchill had been against appeasement. He warned that Germany would take over Europe. In fact, he said, "An appeaser is one who feeds a crocodile, hoping it will eat him last."

Churchill is best known for his inspiring speeches that helped boost the people's morale (their spirit). He was also integral in convincing the Soviet Union and the US to join the Allies. He knew the war would be lost without them.

One of Churchill's most famous speeches is known as "We shall fight on the beaches." You can find an extract below:

"We shall defend our Island, whatever the cost may be, we shall fight on the beaches, we shall fight on the landing grounds, we shall fight in the fields and in the streets, we shall fight in the hills; we shall never surrender."

A photo of Sir Winston Churchill.
https://commons.wikimedia.org/w/index.php?curid=9479764

Charles de Gaulle

Charles de Gaulle (gall) was a significant figure in France during the war. He had fought in WWI. He was even a prisoner of war. Charles went on to become a colonel in the French Army. During the start of WWII, Charles rose to become a brigadier general. When Germany invaded France, he disagreed with the government's decision to surrender. He wanted France to fight! He fled to England and set up a political party called *Free France*.

Charles made speeches urging the people of France to resist occupation and rise up against the Germans. Because of this, the French government declared him a traitor and sentenced him to death. Luckily, this never happened. Charles continued to run the French Resistance. He and his men took part in D-Day and helped liberate Paris.

When Germany was forced to hand over France, Charles de Gaulle took over as the interim leader and helped France reestablish its government. He was later elected as president of France in 1958.

Fun Fact: Although they were allies, Charles de Gaulle did not get along with Winston Churchill or Franklin Delano Roosevelt.

Fun Fact: President Franklin Roosevelt was the thirty-third president of the United States. Joseph Stalin was the leader of the Soviet Union during the war.

Chapter 7 Challenge Activity

Can you unjumble these definitions to match them with their correct phrases?

The Blitz	A government led by an oppressive, nationalist, or racist dictator with complete control.
D-Day	A method of keeping the peace through negotiation
Führer	The allied powers of Germany, Italy, and Japan
The Third Reich	An extensive bombing campaign by the Germans on London
The Axis Powers	Another name for Nazi Germany
Appeasement	The German word for leader that now has strong associations with Hitler
Fascism	The Invasion of Normandy, where the Allies pushed Germany out of France

The Blitz	An extensive bombing campaign by the Germans on London
D-Day	The Invasion of Normandy, where the Allies pushed Germany out of France
Führer	The German word for leader that now has strong associations with Hitler
The Third Reich	Another name for Nazi Germany
The Axis Powers	The allied powers of Germany, Italy, and Japan
Appeasement	A method of keeping the peace through negotiation
Fascism	A government led by an oppressive, nationalist, or racist dictator with complete control

Chapter 8: The Holocaust

The Holocaust (ho-luh-kawst) took place during World War II. The Holocaust remains one of the most horrific events in human history. Under Adolf Hitler's instruction, the Nazis killed anyone he didn't like. He especially targeted the Jews. Around six million Jewish men, women, and children were killed during the Holocaust. Other groups were also singled out by the Nazis, such as Polish people, Serbians, black people, the Romani, gay people, people with disabilities, and Catholics. It is estimated that the Nazis were responsible for murdering up to seventeen million people.

The Nazis believed that Jewish people were less than human and blamed them for many of Germany's problems, including WWI. Hitler thought that the *Aryan race* was superior. The Aryan race doesn't actually exist, but Hitler believed Aryans were non-Jewish Germans with qualities he admired, such as white skin, blonde hair, and blue eyes.

In 1925, Hitler wrote a book called *Mein Kampf* ("My Struggle"). He described how he wanted to rid Germany of every Jew in his book. Few people believed he would really do this. But as soon as he rose to power, he began stripping the Jews of their rights. Then, on November 9th, 1938, during the *Night of Broken Glass*, many Jewish *synagogues* (places of worship), homes, and businesses were ransacked and burned to the ground.

By the time WWII started, Jewish people could not have businesses or go to school. They had to wear the six-pointed Star of David on an armband to show they were Jewish. The Jewish people of Germany and conquered countries were forced to live in ghettos.

Jewish couple with Star of David armbands.

The Nazis didn't stop there. They started rounding up the Jewish people to send them to *concentration camps* as part of their *Final Solution*, which aimed to kill all Jews. The death camps were mostly in Poland. The most notorious one was called *Auschwitz (owsh-vuhts)*.

The concentration camps were similar to prison camps. The people lived in horrific conditions. The trains to the death camps were also deadly. People would be packed in for hours or even days without food or water. Many did not survive the journey. When they arrived, they were separated from their loved ones. They were stripped of all their belongings, and their heads were shaved. They were also given a tattoo of a number that would be used instead of their name. Then, they were forced to do back-breaking hard labor.

Many died from starvation or the cold. The Nazi guards could also kill them if they could not work anymore. Some camps also had gas chambers, where they would kill thousands of people using poison gas. The bodies would be buried in mass graves or burned in huge crematoriums.

Many people did not know what was happening in the concentration camps, but the Jewish people knew they were not nice places. Many Jews tried to hide from the authorities with non-Jewish families. Sometimes, they pretended to be part of the family. Often, they were forced to hide in basements, secret rooms, or attics. Some people were lucky enough to be smuggled out of the country after years of hiding, but many were not.

Perhaps the most famous Jewish person who hid from the Nazis was *Anne Frank*. Anne was a fifteen-year-old girl who hid in a neighbor's attic with her family for two years before they were eventually captured. Like many girls her age, Anne kept a diary. Tragically, Anne did not survive the concentration camp, but her diary did. It is an amazing look into what life was like during WWII. Books that opposed Nazi ideals were often burned. *The Diary of a Young Girl* is read all over the world today. It serves as a sad reminder of the horrible events of the Holocaust.

A photo of Anne Frank
https://commons.wikimedia.org/w/index.php?curid=68542166

Another famous figure of the Holocaust was a German businessman named *Oskar Schindler (o-skuh shind-luh)*. He saved 1,200 Jews who worked for him in Nazi-occupied Poland. In Hungary, a Swedish man named *Raoul (rah-ool) Wallenberg* saved around 100,000 Jews. There are many more incredible stories of the brave people persecuted during the Nazi regime and those who tried to help them.

When the Allies won the war, they *liberated* (freed) the prisoners in the concentration camps. People were horrified when they learned the truth of what had happened. Some Nazi leaders were put on trial and punished for their crimes. Today, we remember the Holocaust in the hopes that we can prevent anything like this from happening again.

Children being liberated from a concentration camp at the end of the war.

Chapter 8 Challenge Activity

1. What was the main group of people that Hitler and the Nazis persecuted?

2. Where were most of the concentration camps located?

3. Who wrote a famous diary of her experience hiding in an attic from the Nazis?

4. What symbol were Jewish people made to wear to show they were Jewish?

5. What was tattooed on people at the concentration camps?

Chapter 8 Answer

1. What was the main group of people that Hitler and the Nazis persecuted? The Jews.

2. Where were most of the concentration camps located? In Poland.

3. Who wrote a famous diary of her experience hiding in an attic from the Nazis? Anne Frank.

4. What symbol were Jewish people made to wear to show they were Jewish? The six-pointed Star of David.

5. What was tattooed on people at the concentration camps? A number that was used instead of their name.

Chapter 9: Europe in the 20th and 21st Centuries

Europe underwent many changes after World War II. Lots of the countries that the Germans had occupied reestablished their previous governments. Germany was divided into two parts. Western Germany was under the control of the Allies. Eastern Germany was controlled by the Soviet Union (the USSR). The USSR also took over many other Eastern European countries, including Poland, Bulgaria, Romania, Czechoslovakia, Hungary, and Albania. Many buildings, bridges, and roads had been destroyed throughout Europe, so the countries had to rebuild.

Fun Fact: The Allies did not want another world war. They formed the United Nations on October 24th, 1945. It consisted of fifty nations and five permanent Security Council members. The five members were the UK, the US, the USSR, China, and France.

Europe became divided between the *Eastern Bloc* nations, which the communist USSR ruled. The communist Eastern countries formed an alliance called the *Warsaw Pact*. The Western countries and the US formed an agreement against communism known as *NATO*.

Fun Fact: Communism is the political ideal that society should be completely equal. Everyone should be the same, and no one can own more than others. In a communist country, the state owns everything. The Marxist ideals behind communism don't seem to work in practice. People often have less freedom and are forbidden from practicing religion. They have little rights over where they live or what they do for work. There is often corruption within the government. Communist governments tend to be ruled by dictators.

EASTERN BLOC AREA BORDER CHANGES 1938 TO 1948

- USSR 1938
- Annexed or Expanded SSRs
- Satellite States
- New Satellite State Land
- — 1938 Borders
- — New Borders

FINNISH SSR
RSFSR
ESTONIAN SSR
RUSSIAN SFSR
LATVIAN SSR
LITHUANIAN SSR
RFSFR
BYELORUSSIAN SSR
REP. OF POLAND
GERMANY (Soviet-zone)
UKRAINIAN SSR
CZECHOSLOVAK REP.
MOLDAVIAN SSR
AUSTRIA (Soviet-zone)
REP. OF HUNGARY
ROMANIAN PEOPLE'S REP.
FEDERAL PEOPLE'S REP. OF YUGOSLAVIA
PEOPLE'S REP. OF BULGARIA
PEOPLE'S REP. OF ALBANIA

A map of post-war Europe and the Eastern Bloc.

The communist East and the capitalist West became engaged in an arms race known as the *Cold War*.

Fun Fact: Even though it is called the Cold War, it never became a full-blown war. People were worried that atomic bombs would be used, so the two sides never directly confronted each other.

America and the Soviet Union both competed to own the most nuclear weapons. They spent billions of dollars trying to stockpile as many nuclear arms as possible. Although the US had developed and even used a nuclear bomb during WWII, people were shocked when the Soviets successfully tested their first atomic bomb in 1949. In response, the US created the first hydrogen bomb (an even more powerful bomb) in 1952. The Soviets were close on their heels and created their first hydrogen bomb only a year later.

Fun Fact: China, Great Britain, and France all joined in the arms race. They developed their own nuclear weapons during the Cold War.

Next, the countries tried to outdo each other by creating *intercontinental ballistic missiles (ICBMs)*. These missiles had a very long range. A country wouldn't even need to be close to drop an atomic bomb!

People all over the world began to worry about what would happen if a nuclear weapon was used. The US and the USSR could destroy each other even if they were hit first. This was called *mutually assured destruction (MAD)*. Because of this, neither side ever used its weapons. The risk was just too great.

Fun Fact: By the 1960s, there were enough nuclear weapons to destroy the world!

The cost of the arms race was very expensive. By the 1970s, both sides began to ease production. The Soviet Union was spending over a quarter of its budget on the military, which greatly impacted its economy. However, the Cold War didn't fully end until the collapse of the Soviet Union in 1991.

Fun Fact: The Cold War lasted for forty-five years!

When Germany was divided into two after World War II, Berlin, the capital city, was also split in half, even though it was technically located in the East. Not everyone in the communist East wanted to be there, so many people fled to live on the Western side of Berlin. In 1961, the government of Eastern Germany decided to build a wall to separate East and West Berlin. They felt it was too easy for people to get into West Berlin, and they were losing too many people.

Fun Fact: From 1949 to 1959, over two million people moved from East to West Germany. Another 230,000 people left in 1960 alone!

The *Berlin Wall* was made from concrete. It was twelve feet high and four feet wide. Guards stationed along the top of the wall were ordered to shoot anyone trying to go past it. The wall stood for twenty-eight years. Many people still tried to cross it. Around five thousand people successfully escaped past the wall, but an estimated two hundred people lost their lives trying.

In 1985, *Mikhail Gorbachev (mi-kile gaw-buh-chov)* was elected the general secretary of the Soviet Union. He introduced two new reforms. One was for the Soviet Union's restructuring. The other allowed greater freedom of speech. People used this newfound freedom to report on issues and protest. Many states began expressing a desire to become independent. Over time, the Soviet Union began to crumble.

In 1989, a series of revolutions happened throughout the Eastern Bloc. More and more states began demanding their independence. On November 9th, 1989, it was announced that the border between East and West Germany was open. People took to the streets in Berlin and tore down the Berlin Wall in celebration. The following year, Germany was finally reunited as one country.

On Christmas Eve, 1991, the Soviet Union was dissolved and split into fifteen different countries. It was decided that Russia would be the "successor" state. This meant that Russia maintained control of the USSR's nuclear weapons and its seat on the United Nations Security Council.

A photo of people from West and East Berlin on top of the Berlin Wall celebrating its fall on November 9th, 1989.

After WWII, Europe introduced many treaties to try and establish strong bonds between European countries. What we know today as the *European Union (EU)* started in 1957 as an alliance of six European countries: France, Belgium, Germany, Italy, the Netherlands, and Luxembourg. More treaties were agreed upon over the year. In 1993, the *Maastricht (maa-struhkt) Treaty* formally established the *European Union*. By then, six more members had joined: Great Britain, the Republic of Ireland, Greece, Spain, Portugal, and Denmark. Today, there are twenty-seven member states of the European Union.

Fun Fact: In 2016, the United Kingdom voted to leave the EU. It was a very close vote, with 52 percent of people voting to leave and 48 percent voting to stay. While the UK is still part of Europe, they no longer follow all of the EU's rules.

The EU is governed by the European Parliament, the European Council, and the European Commission. They decide on rules and guidelines that EU countries must follow. People who live within the EU can trade freely and move around easily between states.

Fun Fact: The members of the EU share a common currency called the euro.

The flag of the European Union.
https://commons.wikimedia.org/w/index.php?curid=2615952

Europe has not managed to avoid further war since WWII. As of this writing, Ukraine and Russia are at war. The war began in February 2014 and escalated when Russia invaded Ukraine on February 24th, 2022. The war has become the biggest war in Europe since the Second World War. Russian President *Vladimir Putin (vla-duh-meeuh poo-tn)* ordered the invasion of Ukraine and its capital *Kyiv (kee-ev)*. One of the reasons he did this was because Ukraine wanted to join NATO.

It is impossible to tell what the future has in store for Europe. Learning about the past allows you to understand more about what is happening today. Check out our recommendations at the end of this book.

Chapter 9 Challenge Activity

Can you solve the crossword using the clues below?

1. The currency used by states in the European Union

2. This separated the two sides of the German capital

3. The political ideal that the Soviet Union and Eastern Bloc believed in

4. During the Cold War, America and the Soviet Union were in an...

5. Countries had these weapons during the Cold War

6. The alliance between Western Europe

	3	C			2						
		O			B						
		M		1	E	U	R	O			
		M			R						
		U			L					6	
		N			I					N	
		I		5	N	U	C	L	E	A	R
4		S			W					T	
A	R	M	S	R	A	C	E			O	
					L						
					L						

If you want to learn more about tons of other exciting historical periods, check out our other books!

VOL. 1
EUROPEAN HISTORY
FOR KIDS

A CAPTIVATING GUIDE TO THE EARLY HISTORY OF EUROPE FROM PREHISTORIC TIMES, THROUGH ANCIENT EUROPE AND THE MIDDLE AGES, TO THE RENAISSANCE AND THE AGE OF DISCOVERY

CAPTIVATING HISTORY

References

If you've enjoyed this book and would like to expand your knowledge of history, please check out our range of Captivating History books for kids. We also highly recommend the below resources for further reading and viewing.

Websites

www.natgeokids.com

www.kids.britannica.com

Books

Horrible Histories - available on Amazon and at many major book retailers

Simple History - available on Amazon or at

https://simplehistory.co.uk/books/

The Diary of Anne Frank (or *Diary of a Young Girl*)

Goodbye Mr. Tom by Michelle Magorian

YouTube Channels

Simple History https://www.youtube.com/c/Simplehistory

Crash Course https://www.youtube.com/c/crashcourse

TED-ed https://www.youtube.com/teded